MW00940813

THE TRUTH ABOUT CHRISTMAS

Clarence Jackson, Jr.

Glendon Jones, Jr. M.Ed., editor

iUniverse, Inc.
New York   Bloomington

The Truth About Christmas

iUniverse books may be ordered through booksellers or by contacting:

iUniverse
1663 Liberty Drive
Bloomington, IN 47403
www.iuniverse.com
1-800-Authors (1-800-288-4677)

ISBN: 978-1-4401-1064-1 (sc)
ISBN: 978-1-4401-1065-8 (ebook)

Printed in the United States of America

iUniverse rev. date: 01/06/2009

THE TRUTH ABOUT CHRISTMAS

And ye shall know the truth, and the truth shall
make you free.

(John 8:32)

Contents

INTRODUCTION

When I was a child I loved Christmas and looked forward to it each year with great anticipation. I loved watching the parades and Christmas cartoons on television. I enjoyed seeing the decorations in the department stores and around the neighborhoods. When I was in elementary school my classmates and I drew each others names out of a box or a hat. The person's name you drew out of the hat or box; you were supposed to buy him or her a present. You were not supposed to tell the person whose name you drew that you had his name. Just before the holiday break, usually at our class party, we would give the person whose name we drew their present.

At church we the congregation would sing Christmas carols the entire season. We would have a Christmas play also. One year my mother was the director of our Christmas play. It was about the birth of Jesus. I played the inn keeper who told Joseph that there wasn't any room in the inn for him and Mary.

My parents would decorate the inside and outside of our home. It looked so pretty with all the decorations lit up and our aluminum tree in front of the window. My brothers, sister and I would look through the Christmas catalogs and choose the toys, clothes, etc. we wanted Santa Claus to bring to us. My younger brother and I kept our bedroom messy about 99% of the year. However, a few days before Christmas we'd give it a thorough cleaning because we didn't want Santa to come to our home and find our room looking like a disaster area and not leave us any presents. I would tie a rope to my bed post with knots tied on it counting down the days until Christmas. Each day I would untie a knot showing how many days were left. We (my brother, sister and I) would sing carols to put us and keep us in the holiday spirit. Also, during that time we would go on a scavenger hunt for any presents hidden around the house. One year my parents were in the living room sitting on the sofa watching television. My brother crawled under the in table and found what we thought were our presents hidden behind the sofa. My parents told us that Santa knew we'd be looking for them so he put empty packages resembling our gifts behind the sofa.

When Christmas Eve arrived we would put out milk and cookies for Santa and get to bed early because our parents told us if Santa came and caught us awake he'd put pepper in our eyes. My brother was usually the first one to awaken very early on Christmas morning. He'd call to me to awaken me and we'd see our stockings full of candy, nuts and fruit hanging from our bed. We would rush into the living room and tear into our presents. We never ate breakfast, lunch or dinner that entire day. We just played with our toys and ate candy, fruit and nuts. To me those were the best Christmases ever.

When I grew older I still looked forward to the Christmas season. I didn't look for Santa anymore or toys but I still loved the season and what it brought with it (the decorations, sometimes snow, family and friends coming in for Christmas dinner, taking photos of each other, etc.). After I accepted Jesus Christ as my personal Lord and savior I had a new excitement about Christmas.

I was celebrating my savior's birth. The presents we gave to each other reminded me of the gift of God's only begotten son who came to be the savior of the world (John 3:16).

However, soon after I was born again I was told by some well meaning Christians that the celebration of Christmas was not for God's children and I should not participate in it. I was also told that it was not the savior's birthday. It was nothing more than a pagan (non-Christian) ritual and too commercialized (exploited for profit). I was even quoted biblical scripture references regarding that fact. I heard about a Bishop who goes on vacation every December and travels so he doesn't have to be involved in the celebration of the most important birth this world or any other world has ever known. Just because the world has taken something sacred and made it pagan and commercialized, doesn't mean that we (Christians) should not celebrate it. The only thing we have to do is not adopt the same attitude as the world has done.

It just seemed totally absurd to me that we who claim to know God, and accept the sacrificial death, burial, and resurrection of his son the Lord Jesus Christ, would not want to go all out in the celebration of his birth. After all, it seems to me that Jesus' birth is as important as his death; for had he not been born we who claim to be born again are still in our sins and on our way to hell.

I was watching a televangelist on a Christian television station one morning teaching on the subject of Christmas. When I heard what his message was going to be about I grabbed my pen and paper to take notes, and to write down ordering information in case I wanted to purchase a copy of it. It seemed as though the Lord had the broadcast on at the right time, and had me in the right place to hear and receive the message. He explained many things in his message about Christmas. He gave me enough information to get started on my own exhaustive search. While researching this topic, I discovered I had always read the Bible from a "traditional" point of view. What I mean is I read the Bible concerning the birth of Jesus from what I was told and seen depicted, and not from what it actually says. Since I read the Bible in reference to Christmas from this traditional viewpoint, I came to the conclusion that there may be other people who also probably read it from this perspective as well.

I ask you the reader to set aside any preconceived ideas regarding Christmas, and approach this study with an open mind. May I also suggest that you have your Bible open to see for yourself what the Word of God says and not just take my word for it as we have done, and unfortunately, are still doing in the secular and the Christian world.

1

THE BIRTH OF JESUS CHRIST

MATTHEW 1:18-25

18 Now the birth of Jesus Christ was on this wise: When as his mother Mary was espoused to Joseph, before they came together, she was found with child of the Holy Ghost.

19 Then Joseph her husband, being a just man, and not willing to make her a public example, was minded to put her away privily.

20 But while he thought on these things, behold, the angel of the Lord appeared unto him in a dream, saying, Joseph, thou son of David, fear not to take unto thee Mary thy wife: for that which is conceived in her is of the Holy Ghost.

21 And she shall bring forth a son, and thou shalt call his name JESUS: for he shall save his people from their sins.

22 Now all this was done, that it might be fulfilled which was spoken of the Lord by the prophet, saying,

23 Behold, a virgin shall be with child, and shall bring forth a son, and they shall call his name Emmanuel, which being interpreted is, God with us.

24 Then Joseph being raised from sleep did as the angel of the Lord had bidden him, and took unto him his wife:

25 And knew her not till she had brought forth her firstborn son: and he called his name JESUS.

The book of Matthew says that Mary, who was to be the mother of Jesus, was engaged to Joseph. Before they were married the Word of God (Matthew 1:18) says that Mary was found with child; meaning she was pregnant. The Word goes on to say that Mary and Joseph had not known each other intimately. So, the child she was carrying was not Joseph's biologically. He didn't want to make her a public example for what had happened. He was contemplating what he should do about the situation. The angel of the Lord appeared to him in a dream assuring him that he should not be afraid to take Mary as his wife because what had happened to her was the result of the Holy Ghost.

Verse twenty-three says **Behold, a virgin shall be with child.** Mary was a virgin when Jesus was conceived. But, after she gave birth to him she did not stay a virgin. Some religions still believe that she is a virgin. But according to the Word of God that isn't true. Let's look at it more closely and in the light of other scriptures.

Joseph took Mary for his wife and they did not consummate their union until after she gave birth to her *firstborn* son (Jesus). The word *firstborn* means that there had to be at least a second born; meaning that Mary had more than one child. Otherwise, the Bible would not have mentioned it. My parents had four children. My older brother was adopted. I am their *firstborn* flesh and blood son, because after I was born they had another son and even a daughter. My younger brother has one child, a daughter. He nor anyone in our family refers to her as

2

"firstborn" because she isn't. She is the only born. I submit to you that after Mary gave birth to Jesus, Joseph didn't wait very long to consummate their union.

Since the Word of God states that Mary and Joseph had more children, which means she was no longer a virgin, let's take a look at some more scriptures which leave no room for doubt that Mary had more than one child:

MATTHEW 13:53-56

53 And it came to pass, that when Jesus had finished these parables, he departed thence.
54 And when he was come into his own country, he taught them in their synagogue, insomuch that they were astonished, and said, Whence hath this man this wisdom, and these mighty works?
55 Is not this the carpenter's son? Is not his mother called Mary? And his brethren, James, and Joses, and Simon, and Judas?
56 And his sisters, are they not all with us? Whence then hath this man all these things?

Jesus had just finished teaching in parables about the sower in relation to God's kingdom. He departed and came back into his own hometown and taught in the synagogue. While he was teaching, the people were astonished at his sayings and the mighty works he performed. When he was living at home it appears that he wasn't performing any miracles or speaking with such wisdom. This happened after he left his hometown. They asked the question was he not the son of Joseph the carpenter and Mary. Now, pay attention to what they asked next. They asked if his brothers and sisters were not living in the same hometown as they were. If Mary and Joseph had not had any more children the town's people would never have said it. So, we see from these two accounts that Mary had not only more than one son, but she also had daughters. I reiterate that Jesus was not an only child. And after his birth Mary was no longer a virgin.

MATTHEW 2:1-21

1 Now when Jesus was born in Bethlehem of Judaea in the days of Herod the king, behold, there came wise men from the east to Jerusalem,

2 Saying, Where is he that is born King of the Jews? for we have seen his star in the east, and are come to worship him.

3 When Herod the king had heard these things, he was troubled, and all Jerusalem with him.

4 And when he had gathered all the chief priests and scribes of the people together, he demanded of them where Christ should be born.

5 And they said unto him, In Bethlehem of Judea: for thus it is written by the prophet,

6 And thou Bethlehem, in the land of Juda, art not the least among the princes of Juda: for out of thee shall come a Governor, that shall rule my people Israel.

7 Then Herod, when he had privily called the wise men, inquired of them diligently what time the star appeared.

8 And he sent them to Bethlehem, and said, Go and search diligently for the young child; and when ye

have found him, bring me word again, that I may come and worship him also.

9 When they heard the king, they departed; and, lo, the star, which they saw in the east, went before them, till it came and stood over where the young child was.

10 When they saw the star, they rejoiced with exceeding great joy.

11 And when they were come into the house, they saw the young child with Mary his mother, and fell down, and worshipped him: and when they had opened their treasures, they presented unto him gifts; gold, and frankincense, and myrrh.

12 And being warned of God in a dream that they should not return to Herod, they departed into their own country another way.

13 And when they were departed, behold, the angel of the Lord appeared to Joseph in a dream, saying, Arise, and take the young child and his mother, and flee into Egypt, and be thou there until I bring thee word: for Herod will seek the young child to destroy him.

14 When he arose, he took the young child and his mother by night, and departed into Egypt:

15 And was there until the death of Herod: that it might be fulfilled which was spoken of the Lord by the prophet, saying, Out of Egypt have I called my son.

16 Then Herod, when he saw that he was mocked of the wise men, was exceeding wroth, and sent forth, and slew all the children that were in Bethlehem, and in all the coasts thereof, from two years old and under, according to the time which he had diligently inquired of the wise men.

17 Then was fulfilled that which was spoken by Jeremy the prophet, saying,

18 In Rama was there a voice heard, lamentation, and weeping, and great mourning, Rachel weeping for her children, and would not be comforted, because they are not.

19 But when Herod was dead, behold, an angel of the Lord appeareth in a dream to Joseph in Egypt,

20 Saying, Arise, and take the young child and his mother, and go into the land of Israel: for they are dead which sought the young child's life.

21 And he arose, and took the young child and his mother, and came into the land of Israel.

Matthew 2:1-2 says that wise men from the east, being led by a star, followed it until it rested over Jerusalem. Down through the years we have assumed that the star the wise men followed to Jerusalem was an actual "star" in the evening sky. However, the star could very well have been an angel moving along with them until they came to where Jesus was. You may be wondering where I came up with this assumption. I got it from the Word of God.

JOB 38:1-7
1 Then the Lord answered Job out of the whirlwind, and said,

2 Who is this that darkeneth counsel by words without knowledge?

3 Gird up now thy loins like a man; for I will demand of thee, and answer thou me.

4 Where wast thou when I laid the foundations of the earth? Declare, if thou hast understanding.
5 Who hath laid the measures thereof, if thou knowest? Or who hath stretched the line upon it?
6 Whereupon are the foundations thereof fastened? Or who laid the corner stone thereof?
7 When the morning stars sang together, and all the sons of God shouted for joy?

Also, one of Satan's names before he fell was "the bright and morning star." Take a look at Isaiah 14:12: **How art thou fallen from heaven, O Lucifer, son of the morning! How art thou cut down to the ground, which didst weaken the nations!** In the Hebrew text "son of the morning" means "the morning star." So, as I stated before, there is a very good possibility that the wise men were led to Jesus by an angel.

Herod was distressed over the news from the wise men, that there was another king on the scene besides him. So, he gathered all the chief priests and scribes together and demanded of them where Christ was to have been born. After the chief priests and scribes told the king what was written in the scriptures, he privately called the wise men to talk to them about it. He asked the wise men when they first saw the star appear announcing the birth of Jesus. After they told him the exact time the star appeared to them, he told them to go and worship Jesus, then return to him so he could go and worship him also. Herod was lying to the wise men. He wanted them to return to him to tell him where Jesus was living so he could destroy him. Whatever time they told Herod they saw the star it had to have been a year or two ago because

Herod, and the Word of God refer to Jesus as a "young child." He couldn't have been an infant because an infant isn't referred to as a "young child" but a "baby, babe," or an "infant," signifying that the child was at least one to two years of age. So, we can conclude that by the time the wise men arrived in Bethlehem Jesus was probably walking around and may have even been talking.

As we continue reading the rest of this chapter, pay close attention to how the Word of God emphasizes certain words. What I mean is, notice how some words are repeated over and over again. It's as though the Lord knew we would get certain facts confused, and he wanted to make sure we "got it" so to speak. Look if you will at how many times the words "young child" are mentioned in this chapter. They are mentioned eight times. However, no matter how many times God emphasized that, we still have gotten it mixed up.

Let's get back to the wise men's visitation. After they left from Herod they saw the star again. They followed it until it stood over the house (not the stable) where Jesus was residing. I have often seen the wise men depicted in the nativity scene right along with the shepherds, the animals, the stable, Mary and Joseph. They were **NOT** at the stable. They came on the scene about a year or two later. I have also seen Christmas cards showing the wise men at the stable. That is a scripturally inaccurate depiction. After Mary gave birth I submit to you that it wasn't long thereafter that Joseph put her and her baby in a house.

I was listening to a well known televangelist talking about Christ's birth and who was present at the stable. His message was very inspirational, but it was also scripturally inaccurate. He read the scripture which stated that Mary, Joseph, the animals, and the shepherds were the **ONLY** ones at the stable when Jesus was born. Yet, immediately after reading the scripture he too said the wise men were also in attendance. He was looking at the savior's birth through his eyes of tradition as many others have and still do.

The Word says in verse one **...there came wise men from the east to Jerusalem.** Notice what the Word does not say: **...there came** *three* **wise men from the east to Jerusalem.** I italicized the word "three" to emphasize the fact that the Bible doesn't say there were "three" wise men. It just says "wise men" with no mention as to the number who came to worship Jesus. Verse 11 says that when the wise men came into the house and saw the young child Jesus they fell down and worshipped him. Then they opened their treasures and presented to him gifts of gold, frankincense, and myrrh. I believe this is where the idea that there must have been only three wise men originated; the first wise man bearing gold, the second wise man bearing frankincense, and the third wise man bearing myrrh. I reiterate, the Word of God doesn't say that there were three wise men. It only says "wise men." We know there was more than one wise man because the Word said "men" which is plural meaning more than one. So, it would not be improper to say that 50 men could've brought gold, 20 men could've brought frankincense, and 10 men could've brought myrrh. Or it could've been two men bearing all three gifts.

Before moving on, there is another fact often overlooked. It is the mode of transportation used by the wise men to travel from the east to Jesus. Nowhere does the

Word say that they traveled by camel back. They could've walked or ridden by horse back for all we know. Yet, when you see nativity scenes or Christmas cards you see the three wise men riding on camels.

We're all familiar with the hymn "We Three Kings." It's a beautiful song but again, nowhere in scripture are the wise men referred to as "kings." According to the Word they were referred to as "wise men," meaning they were educated or scholarly men. Some scholars believe they were religious leaders, philosophical teachers, astrologers and astronomers.

I'm sure some of you are wondering why I'm being so "nitpicky." Well, I believe if I say I am a Christian, and believe and follow the precepts of the Bible, I of all people should strive to be as accurate as possible when it comes to the Word of my Lord. Besides, it doesn't take a born again person to read the Christmas story and figure out that some things we believe and do out of religious tradition are not in the Bible.

The wise men were warned by God in a dream to not return to Herod. So, they went back to their own country another way. Then the angel of the Lord appeared to Joseph in a dream and told him to take the young child, and Mary, and quickly go to Egypt because Herod will be looking for Jesus to kill him. The Word says that Joseph awoke from sleep and took his family into Egypt as he was told to do by the angel of the Lord.

When Herod came to the conclusion that he was double crossed by the wise men; he became very angry. He ordered that all the children from two years old and under that were in Bethlehem and the surrounding coasts be killed. He specifically said only children from two years old and under because he remembered what time the wise men said they saw the star announcing his birth. Since the wise men didn't return to tell him who the child was and where he was, he figured if he had all the children killed in those age groups he would get the right one. So, from this we can deduce that it took the wise men about two years to get to Jesus. Otherwise, Herod would've had all children killed no matter what their ages. This is also proof positive that Jesus was a young child probably walking, and maybe even talking when the wise men got to him. Now, let's take a look at Luke's account of the birth of Jesus:

LUKE 2:1-20

1 And it came to pass in those days, that there went out a decree from Caesar Augustus, that all the world should be taxed.

2 (And this taxing was first made when Cyrenius was governor of Syria.)

3 And all went to be taxed, every one into his own city.

4 And Joseph also went up from Galilee, out of the city of Nazareth, into Judaea, unto the city of David, which is called Bethlehem; (because he was of the house and lineage of David:)

5 To be taxed with Mary his espoused wife, being great with child.

6 And so it was, that, while they were there, the days were accomplished that she should be delivered.

7 And she brought forth her firstborn son, and wrapped him in swaddling clothes, and laid him in a manger; because there was no room for them in the inn.

8 And there were in the same country shepherds abiding in the field, keeping watch over their flock by night.

9 And, lo, the angel of the Lord came upon them, and the glory of the Lord shone round about them: and they were sore afraid.

10 And the angel said unto them, Fear not: for behold, I bring you good tidings of great joy, which shall be to all people.

11 For unto you is born this day in the city of David a Saviour, which is Christ the Lord.

12 And this shall be a sign unto you; Ye shall find the babe wrapped in swaddling clothes, lying in a manger.

13 And suddenly there was with the angel a multitude of the heavenly host praising God, and saying,

14 Glory to God in the highest and on earth peace, good will toward men.

15 And it came to pass, as the angels were gone away from them into heaven, the shepherds said one to another, Let us now go even unto Bethlehem, and see this thing which is come to pass, which the Lord hath made known unto us.

16 And they came with haste, and found Mary, and Joseph, and the babe lying in a manger.

17 And when they had seen it, they made known abroad the saying which was told them concerning this child.

18 And all they that heard it wondered at those things which were told them by the shepherds.

19 But Mary kept all these things, and pondered them in her heart.

20 And the shepherds returned, glorifying and praising God for all the things that they had heard and seen, as it was told unto them.

Caesar Augustus made a decree that the entire world should be taxed. Everyone was to return to his home city for this taxing. Joseph and Mary left from Galilee to go back to Bethlehem. Mary was pregnant and was about to give birth. According to the Word of God, while they were in Bethlehem she gave birth to Jesus.

For years I had always believed that Mary "had" to have her baby in a stable, and "had" to use a manger (stall for animals) for his bed because she and Joseph were so poor they didn't have the money to stay at the local hotel. Unfortunately, this is a belief that a lot of people have. However, it is an inaccurate belief. The Word says nothing at all about Mary and Joseph being poor. Nor does it say that they "had" to go to a stable and use a manger for the birth of Jesus because they could not afford to stay any place else. In fact, it says the opposite. Look again at verse seven. It says that Mary wrapped her son in swaddling clothes (strips of cloth) and laid him in a manger **because there was *no* room for them in the inn.** How would Mary and Joseph know that there wasn't any room in the inn unless they asked first? They had to have asked; otherwise the Word of God would have no reason to mention that.

Let us assume for example, I was going to a city, and when I arrived there I discovered that all the hotels did not have any vacancies. There is only one way I would know that there weren't any vacancies; and that would be if I asked or saw signs posted as I drove up to the hotels that

read "No Vacancies." This also means that I had to have
had the funds to pay for a hotel room or I would have
been an idiot to stop to them when I knew perfectly well
I did not have any money to pay for a night's lodging. Just
like it stands to reason that Mary and Joseph went to the
inn to try to get a room but found out there weren't any
vacancies. This also means that Joseph had the money to
pay for a room. He wasn't flat busted broke as many people
in the secular and Christian world have been inclined to
believe. If he was broke it would have been ridiculous for
him to go to the inn for a room when he knew perfectly
well he did not have the money to pay for it. To quote an
old saying, "How was he going to get it? With his good
looks?" You can bet on it, if there was a vacancy in that
inn Joseph would have snapped it up, and Jesus would
have been born there instead of in a stable.

As we read further in our chapter we see the angel of
the Lord appear to some shepherds in a field watching
over their flock at night. The angel announces to the
shepherds that Jesus is born and tells them they can find
him lying in a manger wrapped in strips of cloth. Pay
special attention if you will, as to whom did not come
to the manger to see the babe: the wise men. The Word
of God says that only the shepherds came to the manger
to see the baby Jesus. And also notice that the Bible did
not say "young child" as the scriptures said in Matthew's
account, but "babe." The word "babe" signifies that Jesus
was a baby or an infant when the shepherds came to see
him.

I do not have a nativity display in my yard at Christmas.
If I were to put a nativity scene in my yard I would make
two displays. The first display would show the nativity

scene with Mary, Joseph, the baby Jesus in the manger, the shepherds and the animals. The second display would show a house with Mary, Joseph, the young child Jesus, and the wise men (more than three). I believe this would be the most accurate way to depict the birth of Jesus and the visitation from the wise men in line with the Word of God. I do display small nativity sets in my home during the Christmas season. I have Mary, Joseph, the baby Jesus, the animals and the shepherds at the manger. I have about four to five wise men coming from the east on their way to the young child, Jesus.

Notes

Notes

2

WAS JESUS BORN ON DECEMBER 25TH?

The question "Was Jesus born on December 25th?" has been a topic of debate for centuries. We do not know exactly for sure when Jesus was born. Many scholars believe he may have been born in the springtime around March or April, at the time of Passover. I ask what difference does it make. If he wasn't born then those of us who claim him as our Lord and Savior are still in our sins and on our way to hell. But, praise God he was born and our (those who are born again) names are written in the Lamb's book of life (Revelation 21:27).

There's an old saying, "we major on minors and minor on majors." What this is saying is that we make such a big deal over things that really don't amount to a "hill of beans" so to speak, and the things that really matter we give them little or no importance at all. God, our heavenly Father, must've figured our knowing the exact date, time and season wasn't all that important, because He didn't mention it in the Bible. The main important fact that was mentioned, and that we should be majoring on, is that Jesus was born so you and I could be born again by his sacrificial death and resurrection. But, since some people like to major on minor things, lets look at a couple of examples and you too will see how unimportant it is.

There is a lady who is a member of my church and is in her 80s. She says that she was born either November

25th or 26th. She really isn't certain. But you know what? She was born. And the proof that she was born is that I can visit her, see her at church, and even talk to her on the telephone. This signifies that she was born and is alive today. She not knowing the exact date of her birth is irrelevant in the light of the fact that she is walking around on this earth like I am. And to top it off she has children, grand children, great grand children, and even great, great grand children to attest to the fact that she was born.

Now, let's take you the reader of this book as another example. Even you don't know when you were born. Let's say, hypothetically, you were born on June 3, 1957, at 2:40 p.m. in Los Angeles, California. I want to ask you two questions. Are you absolutely certain you were born on that date and time? And are you absolutely certain you were born in Los Angeles, California? You're probably saying "Of course, I'm certain. No doubt about it." Well, let me ask you another question. How do you know for certain you were born on June 3, 1957 at 2:40 p.m., and that you were born in Los Angeles, California? Again, you're probably saying you're certain because your birth certificate says you were, and your parents say you were. But do you know what? They could be wrong. You may have been born on June 2, 1957 at 2:40 p.m. in Los Angeles, California. You, from personal experience, have no clue as to when you were born or where. You are only going on information given to you by the doctor who delivered you, and what your parents told you. Since you're probably still saying you know beyond a shadow of a doubt that you were born on this date, time and city, let me say this: I guess when you came out of your mother's womb you looked up at the clock, and a calendar in the delivery room, and said to your mother and the doctor, "Hey Ma, Hey Doctor So and So! I'm here! And it's June 3, 1957 at 2:40 p.m. in the city of Los Angeles." I think you now get the point I'm trying to make. It's not important when you were born. The fact is that you were born, and the indisputable proof of that fact is that you are reading this book.

Now, let's take one last look at Jesus. As we said earlier in our study, since there has been an issue over this fact concerning his birth, some religions and some individuals refuse to celebrate it. Yet, what gets me is, don't you dare forget their birthday. They'll have a conniption. They want a cake, candles, and the works. And if they don't go in for the celebration of it; they will mention it to someone so they can hear that person say "Happy Birthday!" I think if anyone's birthday should be forgotten it should be ours. We didn't die and shed our blood for anyone. Only Jesus Christ alone did that. We should be making a big "to do" over his birth no matter what date it was.

Notes

Notes

3

GIVING GIFTS

When I think about Christmas, my favorite time of the year, I think about the birth of the man who gave his life to redeem me from my sins. I buy gifts and give them at this holy time of year as an expression of my love for him, and for all he has done for me. When I give someone a gift they didn't expect, not just at Christmas but at any time of the year, seeing the joy on his or her face cannot be put into words. The joy on my face, the giver, and the warm feeling in my heart cannot be put into words either. I can imagine how God the Father feels whenever someone accepts His son as their personal savior and Lord.

Not only do I give gifts to others, but I also buy gifts for myself. I gift wrap them and put a bow on them. On the gift tag I write my name as to the person it is for, and I write Jesus' name on it as the giver. The reason I do this is because if it wasn't for him enabling me to have the funds to buy the gifts; I wouldn't have them.

I can think of no better time of the year to give a gift to someone than at Christmas. That person is in a very receptive mood because of the spirit of the season. The best thing of all is, I can give a Christian oriented gift like a book, a plaque, jewelry, etc., to someone who doesn't know Jesus as their personal savior and Lord, and it not appears too "preachy." I have enjoyed giving gifts to people during the Christmas season I had desired to tell about the love of Jesus, but did not know how to go about it. Giving them a gift has opened the door for me to share about him.

You may be wondering where all this gift giving came from in the first place. Let's look in the Bible. The world has made many things sacred seem sacrilegious. And unfortunately, giving gifts is no exception. But God was, and is the author of gift giving. The Bible says in Ephesians 5:1 (Amplified Version), **Therefore be imitators of God [copy Him and follow His example], as well-beloved children [imitate their father].** When I give gifts to people I am following my Father's example. Let's look at some scriptures that show that God is the originator of gift giving.

If ye then, being evil know how to *give* **good** *gifts* **unto your children, how much more shall your Father which is in heaven** *give* **good things to them that ask him (Matthew 7:11)?**

For God so loved the world that he *gave* **his only begotten Son, that whosoever believeth in him should not perish, but have everlasting life (John 3:16).**

Then Peter said unto them, Repent, and be baptized every one of you in the name of Jesus Christ for the remission of sins, and ye shall receive the *gift* **of the Holy Ghost (Acts 2:38).**

For the wages of sin is death; but the *gift* **of God is eternal life through Jesus Christ our Lord (Romans 6:23).**

Now there are diversities of *gifts*, but the same Spirit. For to one is *given* by the Spirit the word of wisdom; to another the word of knowledge by the same spirit; to another faith by the same Spirit; to another the *gifts* of healing by the same Spirit; to another the working of miracles; to another prophecy; to another discerning of spirits; to another divers kinds of tongues; to another the interpretation of tongues (1Corinthians 12:4,8-10):

For by grace are ye saved through faith; and that not of yourselves: it is the *gift* of God (Ephesians 2:8).

Wherefore he saith, When he ascended up on high, he led captivity captive, and *gave gifts* unto men. And he *gave* some, apostles; and some, prophets; and some, evangelists; and some, pastors and teachers; for the perfecting of the saints, for the work of the ministry, for the edifying of the body of Christ (Ephesians 4:8,11-13):

I italicized the words "give, gave, gifts and given" to emphasize that God gave and loves to give us gifts. If anyone should know how to give gifts it's definitely Him. And since I am to imitate Him there can't be anything wrong with me giving gifts either.

Since we're discussing giving gifts to each other at Christmas, have you ever wanted to give a gift to Jesus? I have heard of people placing an empty gift wrapped box under the Christmas tree with a gift tag attached to it with Jesus' name on it. The meaning behind it was you were to fill it with things you could give to Jesus. You may ask what you could possibly give to him. Well, Matthew tells us what we can give as our gift to him.

MATTHEW 25:35-40

35 For I was an hungered, and ye gave me meat: I was thirsty, and ye gave me drink: I was a stranger, and ye took me in:

36 Naked, and ye clothed me: I was sick, and ye visited me: I was in prison, and ye came unto me.

37 Then shall the righteous answer him, saying, Lord, when saw we thee an hungered, and fed thee? Or thirsty, and gave thee drink?

38 When saw we thee a stranger, and took thee in? or naked, and clothed thee?

39 Or when saw we thee sick, or in prison, and came unto thee?

40 And the King shall answer and say unto them, Verily I say unto you, Inasmuch as ye have done it unto one of the least of these my brethren, ye have done it unto me.

By showing love to others by helping them, it is the same as my doing it to Jesus himself. These scriptures should serve as a reminder to do good deeds for others not only during Christmas but every day. I can think of no better gift to give to my savior.

Before I leave this chapter I'd like to reiterate that God isn't opposed to giving gifts. If you will recall, in Matthew 2:11 even the wise men presented to Jesus gifts of gold, frankincense, and myrrh. And no place in the scriptures did God tell them not to give anything to Jesus because it was a heathen ritual or too commercialized. Even Jesus said nothing about the gifts that were given to him by the wise men. If it was not a proper thing to do; I would think that God who was able to show the wise men a star in the east announcing His son's birth, then lead them for two years by it, and then when they arrived in Bethlehem followed it again until it rested over the house where Jesus was; was well able to show them a dream, a star, or some other kind of sign telling them not to give His son any gifts. So, if gift giving is good enough for almighty God it's good enough for me.

Notes

Notes

4

THE TRUTH ABOUT ANGELS

Angels are as much a part of Christmas as the birth of Jesus and the wise men. An angel announced to Mary that she would be the mother of our redeemer:

LUKE 1:26-38

26 And in the sixth month the angel Gabriel was sent from God unto a city of Galilee, named Nazareth,

27 To a virgin espoused to a man whose name was Joseph, of the house of David; and the virgin's name was Mary.

28 And the angel came in unto her, and said, Hail, thou that art highly favoured, the Lord is with thee: blessed art thou among women.

29 And when she saw him, she was troubled at his saying, and cast in her mind what manner of salutation this should be.

30 And the angel said unto her, Fear not, Mary: for thou hast found favour with God.

31 And, behold, thou shalt conceive in thy womb, and bring forth a son, and shalt call his name JESUS.

32 He shall be great, and shall be called the Son of the Highest: and the Lord God shall give unto him the throne of his father David:

33 And he shall reign over the house of Jacob forever; and of his kingdom there shall be no end.

34 Then said Mary unto the angel, How shall this be, seeing I know not a man?

35 And the angel answered and said unto her, The Holy Ghost shall come upon thee, and the power of the Highest shall overshadow thee: therefore also that holy thing which shall be born of thee shall be called the Son of God.

36 And behold, thy cousin Elisabeth, she hath also conceived a son in her old age: and this is the sixth month with her, who was called barren.

37 For with God nothing shall be impossible.

38 And Mary said, Behold, the handmaid of the Lord; be it unto me according to thy word. And the angel departed from her.

Angels also appeared to the shepherds proclaiming that Jesus was born in Bethlehem:

LUKE 2:8-14

8 And there were in the same country shepherds abiding in the field, keeping watch over their flock by night.

9 And, lo, the angel of the Lord came upon them, and the glory of the Lord shone round about them: and they were sore afraid.

10 And the angel said unto them, Fear not: for, behold, I bring you good tidings of great joy, which shall be to all people.

11 For unto you is born this day in the city of David a Saviour, which is Christ the Lord.
12 And this shall be a sign unto you; Ye shall find the babe wrapped in swaddling clothes, lying in a manger.
13 And suddenly there was with the angel a multitude of the heavenly host praising God, and saying,
14 Glory to God in the highest and on earth peace, good will toward men.

We see that angels played a vital role in the birth of our savior. Unfortunately, today angels have become an obsession or cult status. Many people pray to angels. I have even heard of Christian and non-Christian people naming "their" angel or asking their angel what his name is. Then once they obtain it from him; they use it when talking about him or to him.

When I was a child in elementary school, every Valentine's Day I would exchange cards with my classmates. On those cards were pictures drawn of little, fat naked babies with tiny wings shooting a bow and an arrow. Those babies were supposed to have been Cupid shooting his arrow of love into my heart. This to me was how I assumed some angels must have looked.

When I became an adult I was employed for a number of years by a Christian book and gift shop. I had seen many pictures and figurines in the store of what was supposed to have been angels according to the Word of God. However, in my study of the Word of God angels were not at all like the ones I had seen. One day while working at the Christian book and gift shop a picture came in of an angel guarding a little child while he slept at night. I fell in love with that picture, and later purchased it. For the very first time I had seen an angel depicted accurately according to the Word of God. Soon after the picture arrived at the store, and was hanging on the wall behind the cashier's counter, a customer came in, saw the picture, and was horrified. She told me that that wasn't a picture of an angel. She also said she was afraid of it. I told her that that was exactly what a real biblical angel looked like. She just would not accept it. Then she proceeded to tell me how they're sweet with flowers in their hair, wearing beautiful gowns, and holding a bouquet of flowers. I was saddened at her response but not surprised. I knew she was only describing what I and she had seen in pictures and figurines. When I saw in the Word what a biblical angel was really like, I started to view those other angels as wimps and not strong enough to even hold the flowers they were depicted as bearing. And when I thought about Cupid I started to view him as nothing more than a tiny demon. You talk about being horrified! I would hate to think I had a little, fat, naked baby with tiny wings, and a bow and an arrow following me around! It's also ironic that we tend to visualize Satan and his cohorts as all powerful and scary. Yet, we see God's holy angels as weaklings. We need to take a good look at the role angles play and how they are depicted not only in the birth of our savior, but throughout the entire Bible. For the answer we are going to start by looking at Psalm 103:20:

Bless the Lord, ye his angels that excel in strength, that do his commandments, hearkening unto the voice of his word.

Psalm 103:20 states that angels excel in strength, which literally means that angels "surpass" or are "mighty" in strength. This to me is saying that angels are not little, fat naked babies or bearers of flowers. Let's see other verses that confirm this fact:

The Lord knoweth how to deliver the godly out of temptations, and to reserve the unjust unto the day of judgment to be punished: But chiefly them that walk after the flesh in the lust of uncleanness, and despise government. Presumptuous are they, self-willed, they are not afraid to speak evil of dignities. Whereas angels, which are *greater* in *power* and *might*, bring not railing accusation against them before the Lord (2 Peter 2:9-11).

And I saw a *strong* angel proclaiming with a loud voice, Who is worthy to open the book, and to loose the seals thereof (Revelation 5:2)?

And I saw another *mighty* angel come down from heaven, clothed with a cloud: and a rainbow was upon his head, and his face was as it were the sun, and his feet as pillars of fire (Revelation 10:1).

And there was war in heaven: Michael and his angels fought against the dragon; and the dragon fought

and his angels, and prevailed not; neither was their place found any more in heaven. And the great dragon was cast out, that old serpent, called the Devil, and Satan, which deceiveth the whole world: he was cast out into the earth, and his angels were cast out with him (Revelation 12:7-9).

And a *mighty* angel took up a stone like a great millstone, and cast it into the sea, saying, Thus with violence shall that great city Babylon be thrown down, and shall be found no more at all (Revelation 18:21).

I took the liberty of italicizing the words "greater, power, might, strong, and mighty." When you think of these words what image do you see in your mind? I'll tell you what I see. When I think of these words I visualize angels who are so big, broad shouldered, tall, and stronger than the world's strongest man. I envision them being so powerful I can't describe it in words. That's the type of angel the customer saw hanging on the bookstore wall. She saw him as something to be feared. I saw him as someone who I am so glad is in my corner watching over me and protecting me according to Psalm 91 which says, **For He will give His angels [especial] charge over you to accompany and defend and preserve you in all your ways of [obedience and service]. They shall bear you up on their hands, lest you dash your foot against a stone (Amplified Version).**

I want to go back for a moment to Revelation 12:7, and talk about an angel who had a name that was given to us by God in His Word. His name is Michael. Michael is known as an archangel, which means he is a chief or principal angel.

DANIEL 10:10-13

10 And, behold, an hand touched me, which set me upon my knees and upon the palms of my hands.

11 And he said unto me, O Daniel, a man greatly beloved, understand the words that I speak unto thee, and stand upright: for unto thee am I now sent. And when he had spoken this word unto me, I stood trembling.

12 Then said he unto me, Fear not, Daniel: for from the first day that thou didst set thine heart to understand, and to chasten thyself before thy God, thy words were heard, and I am come for thy words.

13 But the prince of the kingdom of Persia withstood me one and twenty days: but lo, Michael, one of the chief princes, came to help me; and I remained there with the kings of Persia.

JUDE 9

Yet Michael the archangel, when contending with the devil he disputed about the body of Moses, durst not bring against him a railing accusation, but said, The Lord rebuke thee.

Michael is commonly known as an "angel of war." When I think of an angel of war the first thing that pops into my mind is an angel who is very, very, powerful beyond what my imagination can conceive of. As we see here, Michael had a special assignment. His assignment was to kick Satan and his cohorts out of heaven. Who do you visualize kicking Satan out of heaven? A little, fat, naked baby with tiny wings holding a bow and an arrow? Or do you visualize an angel with flowers in his hair, wearing a pretty gown, and holding a bouquet of flowers in his arms? Can you imagine that type of an angel kicking Satan out of heaven by beating him with his flowers and talking in a soft wimpy voice? Or do you see a super powerful being stronger than a zillion body builders and wrestlers combined? I don't have to tell you by now what I see. It took some powerful beings to kick Satan and his cohorts out of heaven.

As I stated earlier, people are now praying to and worshipping angels, asking angels their names, and even naming "their" personal angel. What does the Bible or Word of God have to say about this? Well, so far in our study we have only read about three angels whose names were mentioned: Gabriel, Michael and Lucifer who later became known as Satan. Let us see if there are any other references to angels in the Word whose names were mentioned in the scriptures.

JUDGES 13:15-21
15 And Manoah said unto the angel of the Lord, I pray thee, let us detain thee, until we shall have made ready a kid for thee.
16 And the angel of the Lord said unto Manoah, Though thou detain me, I will not eat of thy bread: and if thou wilt offer a burnt offering, thou must offer

it unto the Lord. For Manoah knew not that he was an angel of the Lord.

17 And Manoah said unto the angel of the Lord, What is thy name, that when thy sayings come to pass we may do thee honour?

18 And the angel of the Lord said unto him, Why askest thou thus after my name, seeing it is secret?

19 So Manoah took a kid with a meat offering, and offered it upon a rock unto the Lord: and the angel did wondrously; and Manoah and his wife looked on.

20 For it came to pass, when the flame went up toward heaven from off the altar, that the angel of the Lord ascended in the flame of the altar. And Manoah and his wife looked on it, and fell on their faces to the ground.

21 But the angel of the Lord did no more appear to Manoah and his wife. Then Manoah knew that he was an angel of the Lord.

Manoah's wife was unable to bear children. An angel of the Lord appeared to her and told her that she would conceive a son. He instructed her that she was not to eat anything unclean nor drink wine or any other strong drink. He also told her that no razor should touch his head because he was set aside for the Lord for a specific purpose. Manoah's wife told him what the angel of the Lord told her and she did conceive. Then Manoah prayed and asked God to send the angel again to them so he could instruct them regarding how they should raise the child. God answered Manoah's prayer and the angel came to them again.

When the angel returned Manoah wanted him to stay for a while and have some food. The angel said he would stay but did not want anything to eat. He told Manoah if he was planning to offer a burnt offering he was to offer it to the Lord and not to him. The reason he told Manoah not to offer a burnt offering (which was a form of worship) to him was because he was an angel. We'll see that this is what the angel meant shortly. Manoah did not know at the time the man was an angel. He asked the angel his name, so when he shared the word the angel spake to he and his wife with others, he could, as we say, "give him (the angel) the credit" for his word coming to pass. The angel asked him why he wanted to know his name. He then told him it was secret. It wasn't for Manoah to know. Again, the angel is trying to not have Manoah worshipping him or praising him. Let's look at other scriptures that bear witness to what the angel was saying to Manoah:

HEBREWS 1:1-7,13-14
1 God, who at sundry times in divers manners spake in time past unto the fathers by the prophets,
2 Hath in these last days spoken unto us by his Son, whom he hath appointed heir of all things, by whom also he made the worlds;
3 Who being the brightness of his glory, and the express image of his person, and upholding all things by the word of his power, when he had by himself purged our sins, sat down on the right hand of the Majesty on high;

4 Being made so much better than the angels, as he hath by inheritance obtained a more excellent name than they.

5 For unto which of the angels said he at any time, Thou art my Son, this day have I begotten thee? And again, I will be to him a Father, and he shall be to me a Son?

6 And again, when he bringeth in the first begotten into the world, he saith, And let all the angels of God worship him.

7 And of the angels he saith, Who maketh his angels spirits, and his ministers a flame of fire.

13 But to which of the angels said he at any time, Sit on my right hand, until I make thine enemies thy footstool?

14 Are they not all ministering spirits, sent forth to minister for them who shall be heirs of salvation?

The author of Hebrews is writing about how God made Jesus better than the angels. The writer goes on to ask us, the readers, which of the angels did God say at any time that he was His son, and He would be to him his Father. The answer is He never did. He calls Jesus His son, and He calls Himself Jesus' Father. Then God said for all of His angels to worship His son, Jesus. Notice that God didn't tell Jesus to worship the angels, but told the angels to worship him.

In verse seven we see that God's angels are spirits and they are His ministers. Minister, in the Greek Dictionary of the New Testament means "servant." Let me give you an example that will give you a clearer understanding of this word. When I go to a restaurant, a waiter or a waitress comes to me and takes my order for food. He or she is there to "serve" me. I'm not there to serve them. The words "waiter or waitress" literally means to "wait on or serve." I would not be wrong by saying that the waiter or waitress "ministers" to me. That's what the angels of God do. They wait on or serve God, and His children. When I'm in the restaurant I do not bow down and worship the waiter or waitress. Their job is to serve me. They are to try to the best of their ability to make my dining experience a pleasurable one. This also falls in line with verse fourteen that asks the question, are not all the angels ministering (serving) spirits, who are sent forth by God to minister (serve) for those of us who are His children, and heirs of salvation (deliverance). So, according to the scriptures we have seen so far, it is biblical ignorance of the Word of God to worship, pray to, or name an angel. But, we're not going to stop with just these scriptures. In 2 Corinthians 13:1 the Apostle Paul writing to the church in Corinth states: **This is the third time I am coming to you. In the mouth of two or three witnesses shall every word be established.**

And I fell at his (the angel's) feet to worship him. And he said unto me, See thou do it not: I am thy fellow-servant, and of thy brethren that have the testimony of Jesus: worship God: for the testimony of Jesus is the spirit of prophecy (Revelation 19:10).

And I John saw these things, and heard them. And when I had heard and seen, I fell down to worship

before the feet of the angel which shewed me these things. Then saith he unto me, See thou do it not: for I am thy fellow-servant, and of thy brethren the prophets, and of them which keep the sayings of this book: worship God (Revelation 22:8-9).

The Apostle John was exiled to the Isle of Patmos. While on this island he received the Book of Revelation which talks about the end times and when Christ comes back to earth to set up his kingdom. After John had received these revelations he fell at the feet of the angel who showed him those great and wondrous things. If you'll notice the angel in these three verses tell John not to worship him. He directs him to worship God. He tells John that he is his "fellow-servant," which in the Greek text means "a fellow slave of yours I am." He was saying he is only a messenger, and one who also keeps the Word of God like he, and the prophets. To put it in plain English he was saying "Don't worship me. I am not deserving of it. You worship God. I am nothing more than a messenger and a servant." We now see from the above scriptures that we should not worship, pray to, or name an angel.

Notes

Notes

5

CHRISTMAS TREES

JEREMIAH 10:1-4
**1 Hear ye the word which the Lord speaketh unto you,
O house of Israel:**
**2 Thus saith the Lord, Learn not the way of the
heathen, and be not dismayed at the signs of heaven;
for the heathen are dismayed at them.**
**3 For the customs of the people are vain: for one
cutteth a tree out of the forest, the work of the hands
of the workman, with the axe.**
**4 They deck it with silver and with gold; they fasten it
with nails and with hammers, that it move not.**

The above scriptures seem to be saying that having
trees with decorations on them is acting like heathens
(those who do not know God). I was quoted these verses
by someone explaining why I shouldn't have a decorated
tree in my home nor celebrate Christmas. As I have stated
from the beginning, my goal in my Christian life is to
please my heavenly Father in every way. If Christmas
trees with decorations on them were not something He
approved of I was not about to have them in my home.

The Word of God says to **Study to shew thyself
approved unto God, a workman that needeth not to
be ashamed, rightly dividing the word of truth (2**

Timothy 2:15). This tells me that there is a right way to
study the Word of God, and there's a wrong way. I was
determined that I was going to find the "right way." So,
I asked the Lord to show me what His Word was saying
regarding this.

As I just stated at the beginning of this chapter,
Jeremiah 10 seems to be saying that having trees with
decorations on them is acting like heathens. Let's dissect
these verses and see what they're **really saying** and not
what **we** think they're saying. The Lord is telling Israel not
to learn the way of the heathens because they practiced
things that were ungodly. God was saying that since they
were His people, and were supposed to know His ways,
they were to stay away from the customs of those who did
not. In verses three and four God is saying to Israel that
someone (the heathen) cuts a tree out of the forest with
an axe then fastens it to a stand with nails so it doesn't
move. Then they decorate it with silver and gold. This
sounds exactly like what we do today, doesn't it? After we
buy our tree we do nail it to a wooden tree stand or buy
a metal tree stand to hold it in place so it doesn't move or
fall. Then we decorate it with silver and gold ornaments.
It appears after a careful inspection of the Word that God
is saying He is opposed to decorating trees. But, is this
really what the Lord is saying? The answer to this question
lies in the one verse that wasn't quoted to me but is **very**
important. We need to remember that we are to rightly
divide the word of truth; meaning, we need to also look at
it in its context, and to not just pull out certain scriptures
to use for our own purposes and beliefs.

I believe that verse five (which was not quoted to
me) holds the answer regarding whether God approves

or disapproves of His children decorating and displaying trees in their homes. Let's take a look at it: **They are upright as the palm tree, but speak not: they must needs be borne, because they cannot go. Be not afraid of them; for they cannot do evil, neither also is it in them to do good.** The key point in this verse is, they (trees) cannot speak, and for Israel to not be afraid of them because they do not have the power within them to do evil nor good. Now, I ask you, why would God say such a thing? There's only one reason why He would say that, and that is because they (Israel) were viewing the tree as a living thing. When I say "living," I mean alive like a person, or like a god in this case. Israel was to worship God and God alone. The heathens worshipped trees, golden images, animals, etc. He said they (trees) had to be transported (carried) from place to place because they could not move or walk around. If they were truly a god they would have been able to do those things. God did not say it was sinful or wrong to have a decorated tree. He said what was wrong was cutting it down and decorating it for the purpose of worshipping it.

God is not opposed to my having a decorated tree in my home. What He is opposed to is my bowing down before it and saying "Oh, hail the tree!" or praying to it as if it were Him. After I buy my tree, garnish (decorate) it with tinsel, garlands, gold and silver ornaments, lights, a star on the top, and a tree skirt around the bottom, I do not get down on my hands and knees and say "Oh, Christmas tree, I worship you, I praise you, and I adore you! Long live the tree!" I do not pray to my tree expecting it to answer my prayer. I think a decorated tree is something pretty to look at.

Do you know that the idea to decorate a tree came from God? I know you're asking how in the world I could have gotten the idea from God. He doesn't have a Christmas tree. He doesn't? Well, the next time it snows look outside your home if you live in the country or if you live in the city go to the nearest park and take a look at the trees. What do you see? You see beautiful trees covered in snow and icicles. And if you're fortunate you may see a red cardinal sitting on the top. Tell me; doesn't that look like a decorated Christmas tree? It does to me. What could be prettier than icicles hanging from the branches like ornaments? Have you ever seen icicle ornaments on Christmas trees? Where do you suppose we got the idea to do that? From God of course. And we have snow in cans to spray on our trees and windows. Have you ever seen a holly tree? I have one in my yard. It looks like a Christmas tree with the red berries hanging from it.

It says in Ephesians 5:1 (Amplified Version): **Therefore be imitators of God [copy Him and follow His example], as well-beloved children [imitate their father].** As God's child I am suppose to imitate my Father. When a boy is really young, you will sometimes see him trying to imitate his father by walking like him, tying his shoes like him, imitating him in every way. One of my high school classmates was raised on a farm. He wanted to grow up to be a farmer because his father was one. He joined the "Future Farmers of America" club imitating his father. Guess what? Today he is a farmer. His father is deceased and he is now the proprietor. Since my goal is to be just like my Father also, I want to imitate Him by decorating my tree for one month out of a year.

Notes

Notes

6

DECORATIONS

There is nothing more beautiful to me during the Christmas season than seeing a home decorated with lights, candles in the windows, lights on the hedges, gates, yard, and so on. I also love to see inflatable ornaments and other outdoor items for the season. Unfortunately, some people feel we shouldn't be decorating our homes.

Would you be surprised to learn that decorations are in the Bible, and that God Himself uses what I refer to as "decoration terminology"?

EZEKIEL 16:7-14

7 I have caused thee to multiply as the bud of the field, and thou hast increased and waxen great, and thou art come to excellent *ornaments*: thy breasts are fashioned, and thine hair is grown, whereas thou was naked and bare.

8 Now when I passed by thee, and looked upon thee, behold, thy time was the time of love; and I spread my *skirt* over thee, and covered thy nakedness: yea, I sware unto thee, and entered into a covenant with thee, saith the Lord God, and thou becamest mine.

9 Then washed I thee with water; yea, I thoroughly washed away thy blood from thee, and I anointed thee with oil.

10 I clothed thee also with broidered work, and shod thee with badgers' skin, and I girded thee about with fine linen, and I covered thee with silk.

11 I *decked* thee also with *ornaments*, and I put bracelets upon thy hands, and a chain on thy neck.

12 And I put a jewel on thy forehead, and earrings in thine ears, and a beautiful crown upon thine head.

13 Thus wast thou *decked* with *gold* and *silver*; and thy raiment was of fine linen, and silk, and broidered work; thou didst eat fine flour, and honey, and oil: and thou wast exceeding beautiful, and thou didst prosper into a kingdom.

14 And thy renown went forth among the heathen for thy beauty: for it was perfect through my comeliness, which I had put upon thee, saith the Lord God. (Italics mine)

The Word of the Lord came to Ezekiel telling him to let Jerusalem know that what she was doing was an abomination before Him. The Lord told them how beautiful He had made them, and then they stopped trusting in Him, but trusted in their beauty, and acted like a prostitute. I want you to notice how God describes how beautiful He made Jerusalem. He uses the words "ornaments, skirt, decked, gold, and silver." When you see these words what do they remind you of? I will tell you what they remind me of: Christmas decorations. God deliberately describes the beauty He bestowed on Jerusalem in the form of beautiful decorations.

We have just seen that God uses decoration terminology to describe how He adorned Jerusalem. Now we will take a look at some scriptures that actually describes a place in the Bible that is decorated. Try not to be shocked when you discover what place that is.

REVELATION 21:1-2 & 9-21

1 And I saw a new heaven and a new earth: for the first heaven and the first earth were passed away; and there was no more sea.

2 And I John saw the holy city, new Jerusalem, coming down from God out of heaven, prepared as a bride adorned for her husband.

9 And there came unto me one of the seven angels which had the seven vials full of the seven last plagues, and talked with me, saying, Come hither, I will shew thee the bride, the Lamb's wife.

10 And he carried me away in the spirit to a great and high mountain, and shewed me that great city, the holy Jerusalem, descending out of heaven from God,

11 Having the glory of God: and her light was like unto a stone most precious, even like a jasper stone, clear as crystal;

12 And had a wall great and high, and had twelve gates, and at the gates twelve angels, and names written thereon, which are the names of the twelve tribes of the children of Israel:

13 On the east three gates; on the north three gates; on the south three gates; and on the west three gates.

14 And the wall of the city had twelve foundations, and in them the names of the twelve apostles of the Lamb.

15 And he that talked with me had a golden reed to measure the city, and the gates thereof, and the wall thereof.

16 And the city lieth foursquare, and the length is as large as the breadth: and he measured the city with the reed, twelve thousand furlongs. The length and the breadth and the height of it are equal.

17 And he measured the wall thereof, an hundred and forty and four cubits, according to the measure of a man, that is, of the angel.

18 And the building of the wall of it was of jasper; and the city was pure gold, like unto clear glass.

19 And the foundations of the wall of the city were garnished with all manner of precious stones. The first foundation was jasper; the second, sapphire; the third, a chalcedony; the fourth, an emerald;

20 The fifth, sardonyx; the sixth, sardius; the seventh, chrysolyte; the eighth, beryl; the ninth, a topaz; the tenth, a chrysoprasus; the eleventh, a jacinth; the twelfth, an amethyst.

21 And the twelve gates were twelve pearls: every several gate was of one pearl: and the street of the city was pure gold, as it were transparent glass.

The Apostle John was taken away in the spirit by an angel to heaven. He is describing in the Book of Revelation what he saw. Keep in mind that heaven is God's home. The Apostle John states in verse eleven that the holy Jerusalem's light was like a jasper stone, as clear as crystal. Picture if you will a city whose light is so beautiful it can clearly be seen. Imagine a glass made of crystal. It is so precious, and very, very clear. John also said that the city itself is pure gold like clear glass. This means that you can see right through it as though you were looking through a window pane. Now, that is definitely **PURE** gold. It doesn't have a nick or scratch anywhere. Then he goes on to describe the wall of the city. He says that the wall is jasper and enormous. There are twelve gates that have twelve angels. An angel positioned at each gate. There are three gates on the east, three on the north, three on the south, and three on the west. The wall of the city is built on twelve foundations.

Before we go farther lets talk about the foundations under the wall. The Apostle John states that the wall that surrounds the New Jerusalem is on twelve foundations. One can only imagine how high that wall is. When my brother-in-law, my sister, and their children built their home it was set on one foundation and is made of cement blocks. Again, the Bible says that the wall that surrounds the holy Jerusalem is set on twelve foundations. Get this; it isn't set on twelve high cement blocks but on precious, beautiful, bright, colorful stones. Look back if you will again at verses fifteen through twenty-one.

According to verse fifteen the angel measured the city with a golden reed. That golden reed was a ruler made of gold! It wasn't made of wood, plastic or metal like we have here on the earth. And we are getting bent out of shape (upset) over displaying decorations in and on our homes and in our yards one month out of a year. I once heard about a preacher who had gold doorknobs on the doors of his home. Some members of the body of Christ were getting upset because the man of God had these. They were saying that he was using the donations from the supporters of his ministry to buy them. I can only imagine what those same people will say when they get to heaven and see an angel measuring something with a golden ruler! They'll have a conniption. In verse sixteen we see that the city is about 1,500 miles long, from side to side, and high. Next, we see in verse seventeen the angel measuring the wall of the city. The wall is made of jasper and is about 200 feet.

As we move on to verses nineteen and twenty, try to visualize in your mind the wall and the twelve foundations it is sitting on. Bear in mind that the foundations are twelve separate foundations, one on the top of the other, like putting building blocks one on top of another. The Word says that the foundations of the wall of the Holy Jerusalem are garnished (decorated). God decorated the foundations with beautiful, colorful, flawless, stones. Now, what do we say we are going to do at Christmas time? We say we are going to "decorate" our homes with lights, ornaments, wreaths, inflatable snowmen, nativity scenes, and so forth. I would venture to say that our God loves to decorate.

Let's look at one last verse. In verse twenty-one the Apostle John gives us some more information about the holy Jerusalem. He says the twelve gates are twelve pearls; every gate is made of one giant pearl. Can you imagine twelve gates, each made out of giant pearls? I would have liked to have seen the oysters those pearls came out of! Take a look at the street of the city. It is made of pure gold like transparent glass. We have streets here that are made of concrete or cement and you cannot see through them. I was walking to the United States Post Office one day. While I was walking along, all of a sudden I tripped and almost fell on the sidewalk. The sidewalk was so corroded it was in bits and pieces. I can't visualize the street of heaven looking like that. Just imagine walking on a pure gold, flawless street that is like clear glass. As you're walking you stop for a moment and look down. When you look down you see through it as though you were looking through a clean window pane. About a year ago I had new windows installed in my home. After they were installed I looked through those new windows. It was an awesome sight. They were so clean, and crystal clear. However, my clean, crystal clear windows here on earth pales in comparison to the streets of pure transparent gold.

So, we see that God isn't against decorations. On the contrary, heaven is decorated twenty-four hours a day, seven days a week. And some of us here on earth are having catfits (upset) over a few decorations for about one month or so out of a year. I often wonder what these same people are going to say when they arrive in heaven and see it all lit up brighter and prettier than any Christmas decoration on earth. I wonder if they'll tell God he is acting like a heathen.

The Word of God says in John 8:32, **And ye shall know the truth, and the truth shall make you free.** This is saying that you will know the truth and the truth you "know" (so deep within you that **nothing** can take it away from you) will make you free. When I discovered that my heavenly Father was not opposed to my celebrating His son's birth with a decorated tree and decorations, knowing that truth made me feel so free I couldn't put it into words. After doing an exhaustive search of the Word and seeing in the scriptures that even my Father was into decorating, it gave me a sense of peace and excitement. I say excitement because I now try to go "whole hog" at Christmas. I also love to go to the department stores and be in all the hustle and bustle and joy of the season. I enjoy shopping for gifts for my loved ones and close friends. I try to buy a new ornament to add to my indoor and outdoor decorations each year. When I have finished decorating I love to stand outside at night and watch the decorations all lit up. I am a big kid at heart at that time of the year.

I thank my God for opening His Word up to me through revelation knowledge and through His men and women of God who have taught on this subject. I pray that you the reader will know the freedom I have come to know about this blessed holiday. And I also pray that this truth will draw you into a deeper knowledge and relationship with our Lord and Savior, Jesus Christ as it has me.

Notes

Notes

ABOUT THE AUTHOR

Clarence Jackson, Jr. resides on Maryland's eastern shore. He is a minister and author of the book "Was Jesus A Poor Man?" He holds a Bachelor of Arts Degree from Salisbury University. His books are listed in Books in Print, Google, and Yahoo!, and can be ordered from over 25,000 retail bookstores, the iUniverse Online Bookstore, Amazon.com, Barnes and Noble.com, Barnes and Noble Bookstores, Booksamillion.com, Borders.com, Borders and Borders Express Bookstores, Ingram Book Company and Baker and Taylor Wholesalers. Also available worldwide: Australia, Brazil, Canada, France, Germany, Ireland, Japan, Mexico, New Zealand and the United Kingdom.

To find out more about Clarence and upcoming books by him please visit his website at http://clarencejacksonjr.vpweb.com.

CPSIA information can be obtained
at www.ICGtesting.com
Printed in the USA
BVOW08s1402171017
497893BV00001B/34/P